teacher PLANNER

THIS PLANNER BELONGS TO:

_____

Want free goodies?!

Email us at

prettysimplebooks@gmail.com

Title the email "Teacher Planner!" and let us know that you purchased a Pretty Simple Planner!

Find us on Instagram!

@prettysimplebooks

Questions & Customer Service:
Email us at prettysimplebooks@gmail.com!

Teacher Planner Lesson Planner
©Pretty Simple Planners. All rights reserved. No part of this publication may be reproduced, distributed, or transmitted, in any form or by any means, including photocopying, recording, or other electronic or mechanical methods, without prior written permission of the publisher, except in the case of brief quotations embodied in critical reviews and certain other noncommercial uses permitted by copyright law.

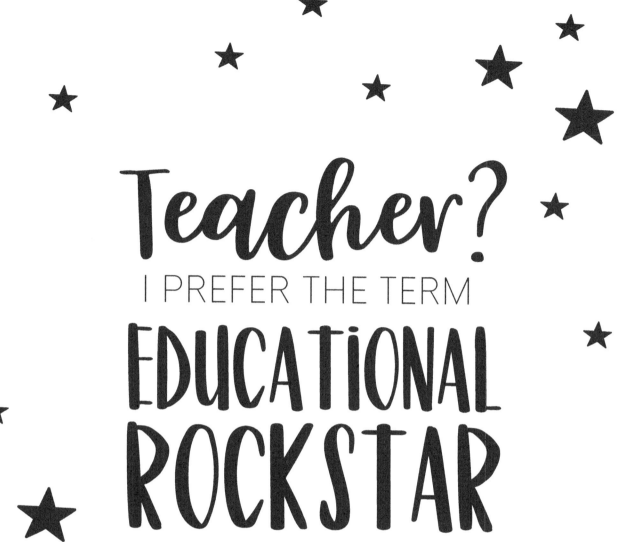

IMPORTANT DATES

January
NEW YEAR'S DAY
MARTIN LUTHER KING DAY

February
GROUNDHOG DAY
VALENTINE'S DAY
PRESIDENTS DAY

March
ST. PATRICK'S DAY

July
INDEPENDENCE DAY

August

September
LABOR DAY

April

- APRIL FOOL'S DAY
- EARTH DAY

May

- CINCO DE MAYO
- MOTHER'S DAY
- MEMORIAL DAY

June

- FATHER'S DAY

October

- COLUMBUS DAY
- HALLOWEEN

November

- VETERANS DAY
- THANKSGIVING

December

- HANUKKAH
- CHRISTMAS EVE
- CHRISTMAS DAY
- NEW YEAR'S EVE

July 2020

SUNDAY	MONDAY	TUESDAY	WEDNESDAY
			1
5	6	7	8
12	13	14	15
19 *National Ice Cream Day*	20	21	22
26	27	28	29

[Live in the sunshine, swim in the sea, drink the wild air.   — Ralph Waldo Emerson]

THURSDAY	FRIDAY	SATURDAY	NOTES
2	3	4 INDEPENDENCE DAY	
9	10	11	
16	17	18	
23	24	25	
30	31		

WEEK OF _____	Monday	Tuesday
SUBJECT:		

Wednesday	Thursday	friday

WEEK OF _____	Monday	Tuesday
SUBJECT:		

Wednesday	Thursday	Friday

WEEK OF _____	Monday	Tuesday
SUBJECT:		

Wednesday	Thursday	Friday

WEEK OF _____	Monday	Tuesday
SUBJECT:		

Wednesday	Thursday	Friday

WEEK OF _____	Monday	Tuesday
SUBJECT:		

Wednesday	Thursday	Friday

August 2020

SUNDAY	MONDAY	TUESDAY	WEDNESDAY
2	3	4	5
9 *Book Lover's Day*	10	11	12
16 *Tell a Joke Day*	17	18	19
23 / 30	24 / 31	25	26 *National Dog Day*

> The secret of getting ahead is getting started.
> — Mark Twain

THURSDAY	FRIDAY	SATURDAY	NOTES
		1	
6 *Root Beer Float Day*	7	8	
13	14	15	
20	21	22	
27	28	29	

WEEK OF _____	Monday	Tuesday
SUBJECT:		

Wednesday	Thursday	Friday

WEEK OF _____	Monday	Tuesday
SUBJECT:		

Wednesday	Thursday	Friday

WEEK OF ____	Monday	Tuesday
SUBJECT:		

Wednesday	Thursday	Friday

WEEK OF _____	Monday	Tuesday
SUBJECT:		

Wednesday	Thursday	Friday

September 2020

SUNDAY	MONDAY	TUESDAY	WEDNESDAY
		1	2
6 *Read a Book Day*	7 LABOR DAY	8	9
13	14	15	16
20	21	22	23
27 YOM KIPPUR	28	29 *National Coffee Day*	30

> With the new day comes new strength and new thoughts.
> - Eleanor Roosevelt

THURSDAY	FRIDAY	SATURDAY	NOTES
3	4	5	
10	11	12	
17	18 ROSH HASHANAH	19	
24	25	26	

WEEK OF _____	Monday	Tuesday
SUBJECT:		

Wednesday	Thursday	Friday

WEEK OF _____	Monday	Tuesday
SUBJECT:		

Wednesday	Thursday	Friday

WEEK OF _____	Monday	Tuesday
SUBJECT:		

Wednesday	Thursday	Friday

WEEK OF _____	Monday	Tuesday
SUBJECT:		

Wednesday	Thursday	Friday

WEEK OF _____	Monday	Tuesday
SUBJECT:		

Wednesday	Thursday	Friday

October 2020

SUNDAY	MONDAY	TUESDAY	WEDNESDAY
4	5	6	7
National Taco Day			
11	12	13	14
	COLUMBUS DAY		
18	19	20	21
25	26	27	28

> Simplicity is the keynote of all true elegance.
> — Coco Chanel

THURSDAY	FRIDAY	SATURDAY	NOTES
1	2 *World Smile Day*	3	
8	9	10	
15	16	17	
22	23	24	
29	30	31 HALLOWEEN	

WEEK OF _____	Monday	Tuesday
SUBJECT:		

Wednesday	Thursday	Friday

WEEK OF _____	Monday	Tuesday
SUBJECT:		

Wednesday	Thursday	Friday

WEEK OF _____	Monday	Tuesday
SUBJECT:		

Wednesday	Thursday	Friday

WEEK OF _____	Monday	Tuesday
SUBJECT:		

Wednesday	Thursday	Friday

November 2020

SUNDAY	MONDAY	TUESDAY	WEDNESDAY
1 DAYLIGHT SAVINGS ENDS	2	3	4
8	9	10	11 VETERANS DAY
15	16	17	18
22	23	24	25
29	30		

> [The purpose of our lives is to be happy.
> — Dalai Lama]

THURSDAY	FRIDAY	SATURDAY	NOTES
5	6	7	
12	13 *World Kindness Day*	14	
19	20	21	
26 THANKSGIVING	27	28	

WEEK OF _____	Monday	Tuesday
SUBJECT:		

Wednesday	Thursday	Friday

WEEK OF _____	Monday	Tuesday
SUBJECT:		

Wednesday	Thursday	Friday

WEEK OF _____	Monday	Tuesday
SUBJECT:		

Wednesday	Thursday	Friday

WEEK OF _____	Monday	Tuesday
SUBJECT:		

Wednesday	Thursday	Friday

December 2020

SUNDAY	MONDAY	TUESDAY	WEDNESDAY
		1	2
6	7	8	9
13	14	15	16
20	21	22	23
27	28	29	30

> What is done in love is done well.
> - Vincent Van Gogh

THURSDAY	FRIDAY	SATURDAY	NOTES
3	4	5	
10	11 HANUKKAH	12	
17	18	19	
24 CHRISTMAS EVE	25 CHRISTMAS DAY	26 KWANZAA	
31 NEW YEAR'S EVE			

WEEK OF _____	Monday	Tuesday
SUBJECT:		

Wednesday	Thursday	Friday

WEEK OF _____	Monday	Tuesday
SUBJECT:		

Wednesday	Thursday	Friday

WEEK OF _____	Monday	Tuesday
SUBJECT:		

Wednesday	Thursday	Friday

WEEK OF _____	Monday	Tuesday
SUBJECT:		

Wednesday	Thursday	Friday

WEEK OF _____	Monday	Tuesday
SUBJECT:		

Wednesday	Thursday	Friday

January 2021

SUNDAY	MONDAY	TUESDAY	WEDNESDAY
		NEW YEAR'S DAY	
3	4 *National Trivia Day*	5	6
10	11	12	13
17	18 MARTIN LUTHER KING JR. DAY	19	20
24 / 31	25	26	27

[Nothing is impossible, the word itself says 'I'm possible'!
- Audrey Hepburn]

THURSDAY	FRIDAY	SATURDAY	NOTES
	1	2	
7	8	9	
14	15	16	
21 *National Hug Day*	22	23	
28	29 *National Puzzle Day*	30	

WEEK OF _____	Monday	Tuesday
SUBJECT:		

Wednesday	Thursday	Friday

WEEK OF _____	Monday	Tuesday
SUBJECT:		

Wednesday	Thursday	Friday

WEEK OF _____	Monday	Tuesday
SUBJECT:		

Wednesday	Thursday	Friday

WEEK OF _____	Monday	Tuesday
SUBJECT:		

Wednesday	Thursday	Friday

february 2021

SUNDAY	MONDAY	TUESDAY	WEDNESDAY
	1	2	3
7	8	9 *National Pizza Day*	10
14 VALENTINE'S DAY	15 PRESIDENTS' DAY	16	17
21	22	23	24
28			

> I have found if you love life, life will love you back.
> — Arthur Rubinstein

THURSDAY	FRIDAY	SATURDAY
4	5	6
11	12	13
18	19	20 *Love Your Pet Day*
25	26	27

NOTES

WEEK OF _____	Monday	Tuesday
SUBJECT:		

Wednesday	Thursday	Friday

WEEK OF _____	Monday	Tuesday
SUBJECT:		

Wednesday	Thursday	Friday

WEEK OF _____	Monday	Tuesday
SUBJECT:		

Wednesday	Thursday	Friday

WEEK OF _____	Monday	Tuesday
SUBJECT:		

Wednesday	Thursday	Friday

March 2021

SUNDAY	MONDAY	TUESDAY	WEDNESDAY
	1	2	3
7	8	9	10
14 **DAYLIGHT SAVINGS BEGINS**	15	16	17 **ST. PATRICK'S DAY**
21	22	23 *National Puppy Day*	24
28	29	30	31

[Anything can happen if you let it.
— Mary Poppins]

THURSDAY	FRIDAY	SATURDAY	NOTES
4	5	6	
11	12	13	
18	19	20 *International day of Happiness*	
25	26	27	

WEEK OF _____	Monday	Tuesday
SUBJECT:		

Wednesday	Thursday	Friday

WEEK OF _____	Monday	Tuesday
SUBJECT:		

Wednesday	Thursday	Friday

WEEK OF _____	Monday	Tuesday
SUBJECT:		

Wednesday	Thursday	Friday

WEEK OF _____	Monday	Tuesday
SUBJECT:		

Wednesday	Thursday	Friday

WEEK OF _____	Monday	Tuesday
SUBJECT:		

Wednesday	Thursday	Friday

April 2021

SUNDAY	MONDAY	TUESDAY	WEDNESDAY
4 EASTER	5	6	7
11	12	13	14
18	19	20	21
25	26 National Pretzel Day	27	28

> The world belongs to the enthusiastic.
> - Ralph Waldo Emerson

THURSDAY	FRIDAY	SATURDAY
1	2 GOOD FRIDAY	3
8	9	10 *National Siblings Day*
15 *National High Five Day*	16	17
22 EARTH DAY	23	24
29	30	

NOTES

WEEK OF _____	Monday	Tuesday
SUBJECT:		

Wednesday	Thursday	Friday

WEEK OF _____	Monday	Tuesday
SUBJECT:		

Wednesday	Thursday	Friday

WEEK OF _____	Monday	Tuesday
SUBJECT:		

Wednesday	Thursday	Friday

WEEK OF _____	Monday	Tuesday
SUBJECT:		

Wednesday	Thursday	Friday

May 2021

SUNDAY	MONDAY	TUESDAY	WEDNESDAY
2 *World Laughter Day*	3	4	5 *Cinco de Mayo*
9 MOTHER'S DAY	10	11	12
16	17	18	19
23 / 30	24 / 31 MEMORIAL DAY	25	26

> Keep your eyes on the stars, and your feet on the ground. — Theodore Roosevelt

THURSDAY	FRIDAY	SATURDAY	NOTES
		1	
6	7	8	
13	14	15	
20	21	22	
27	28	29	

WEEK OF _____	Monday	Tuesday
SUBJECT:		

Wednesday	Thursday	Friday

WEEK OF _____	Monday	Tuesday
SUBJECT:		

Wednesday	Thursday	Friday

WEEK OF _____	Monday	Tuesday
SUBJECT:		

Wednesday	Thursday	Friday

WEEK OF _____	Monday	Tuesday
SUBJECT:		

Wednesday	Thursday	Friday

June 2021

SUNDAY	MONDAY	TUESDAY	WEDNESDAY
		1	2
6	7	8	9
13	14 **FLAG DAY**	15	16
20 **FATHER'S DAY**	21 *World Music Day*	22	23
27	28	29	30

[Adventure is worthwhile in itself.
- Amelia Earhart]

THURSDAY	FRIDAY	SATURDAY	NOTES
3	4	5	
	National Donut Day		
10	11	12	
17	18	19	
24	25	26	

WEEK OF ____	Monday	Tuesday
SUBJECT:		

Wednesday	Thursday	Friday

WEEK OF _____	Monday	Tuesday
SUBJECT:		

Wednesday	Thursday	Friday

WEEK OF _____	Monday	Tuesday
SUBJECT:		

Wednesday	Thursday	Friday

WEEK OF _____	Monday	Tuesday
SUBJECT:		

Wednesday	Thursday	Friday

WEEK OF _____	Monday	Tuesday
SUBJECT:		

Wednesday	Thursday	Friday

STUDENT BIRTHDAYS

January

February

March

July

August

September

April	**May**	**June**

October	**November**	**December**

ATTENDANCE OR GRADE TRACKER

ATTENDANCE OR GRADE TRACKER

ATTENDANCE OR GRADE TRACKER

Made in the USA
Coppell, TX
18 July 2020